My Protocol

My Protocol

How I Broke the Rules and Survived Cancer

Lynda Spinelli

Edited by Michelle Beckman, Sunday Dinner Stories, www.SundayDinnerStories.com.

Back cover photograph courtesy of The Priestley's Fine Art Photography. All other photos supplied by the author.

This book is based on interviews conducted by Michelle Beckman of Sunday Dinner Stories with Lynda Spinelli.

The author has attempted to recreate events, locales and conversations from her memories. In order to maintain anonymity, she changed the names of some individuals and places.

The content of this book is for informational purposes only and is intended to share the author's story of faith, hope, and love. This book is not intended as a substitute for the medical advice of physicians. The reader should regularly consult a physician in matters relating to his/her health and particularly with respect to any symptoms that may require diagnosis or medical attention.

My Protocol / Lynda M. Spinelli—1st edition
ISBN 978-0-6922-6743-1

*To my sons, David and Derek,
and my granddaughter, Evie.
They are the joy of my life.*

Contents

Acknowledgments

Sometimes when your life turns upside down and God sends you on an unexpected journey, you feel like you are alone—lost. But when you look back, you realize that so many people loved you through the journey, a journey that you could not possibly have completed on your own.

To my children and granddaughter—David, Derek, and Evie: All I can say is, love. You loved me unconditionally through my whole ordeal. You mean the world to me!

To my former husband, Joe: I will be forever grateful for your support throughout my diagnosis and treatment and for the loving father you always have been to my children.

To my friends, Nancy and Ethan: Thank God, you did not take *No* for an answer; you saved my life. Thank you for always treating me like a special member of your family. This chapter of my life is complete because of your generosity.

To the designer of the butterfly cross-stitch: Thank you for creating a special design that means so much to me. The picture symbolizes a difficult time in my life when I desperately needed my friends and family. The butterfly represents the transformation that made me the strong, confident woman I am today. I would love to acknowledge you by name. I have contacted craft manufacturers and scoured the Internet looking for any trace of you or your work. If you are reading this, please contact me at Lspin51@gmail.com so I can formally credit your contribution to my story.

To my God: How can I express the level of gratitude I feel? I am so very thankful that You placed the right people in my path at the right time. I am closer to You than I have ever been before, and for that, I am eternally grateful. I truly believe in Your miracles and the divine connections that You orchestrate throughout my life. I am in awe.

Author's Note

I have always been a member of the holistic health community. I practiced yoga. I was a trained massage therapist. I tried to eat well. I avoided medicine as much as possible. I considered myself to be pretty healthy, until I wasn't.

In the year 2000, I was diagnosed with a form of colorectal cancer, rectosigmoid cancer, and I was devastated. I felt lost and alone. I knew traditional treatment was not for me, so I took control of my treatment plan. At times, I was afraid, but I always trusted my gut. I am so glad that I did.

I tell my story because I want cancer patients to know they have choices. Traditional doctors will tell you the *standard* protocol, but humans are not standard, and I don't believe in one-size-fits-all medicine. Patients need to explore their options, trust their inner guidance, and do what is right for them.

The word protocol *reminds me of a time when I was allowed only one option, a time when there was no room for compromise.*

Sometimes a patient, who is thrust into an unexpected illness, can be confused by the terms a doctor uses. I tried to explain some of these terms from a patient's perspective throughout the book and in the Glossary. For example, the term *protocol* refers to the medical community's collective recommendations and regulations for treating a disease or condition. The word *protocol* reminds me of a time when I was allowed only one option, a time when there was no room for compromise. I believed I would die if I followed the *standard* protocol. I felt like I had to take control of my own health and save myself. So I broke the rules, researched all options, and followed my gut. With God's help, I followed *my own* protocol.

When people ask me in person to comment on their treatment plan, their protocol, I always tell them that they need to make their own decisions. Please talk with your physician about the terms he is using and the implications of his recommendations; do your own research; weigh your own options; and make your own choices. Please do not disregard professsional medical advice or delay seeking it because of something you have read in this book. Although I am a nurse, I am not a doctor; nothing in this book should replace the advice of traditional or alternative medical professionals.

> *So I broke the rules, researched all options, and followed my gut. With God's help, I followed my own protocol.*

I have shared candid recollections of my experiences, but please remember that these stories are just that—*my* recollections of *my* experiences in *my* words and in *my* voice. I have done my best to describe each event accurately from my own perspective. Each family member or friend who participated in these events should realize how deeply he or she touched my life. I pray that my experiences will inspire cancer patients to take control of their own health and follow their own protocol.

My Cancer Journey

.

I'll Definitely Teach You

Bright, natural light streamed through the window into Bari Ann's Newton, Massachusetts, living room on a March afternoon in 2001. I loved her warm, cozy, open home. She had beautiful plants in the living room and a white tabby cat roaming the halls. I felt very comfortable there.

Bari Ann took a liking to Japanese decor when she visited her son in Japan a few times. She decorated her home with Asian inspired cross-stitch projects, and I admired them each time I visited. I liked to work with my hands, so one day I said to her, "I would love to learn how to do that!"

She said, "Well, I'll definitely teach you."

I was not surprised when she bought a small, cross-stitch project for me that also had an Asian flair. A few days later, we went to the craft store, and we bought the threads together. The pattern had all the different colors printed on the fabric. We went back to her house, and she started to teach me to cross-stitch.

We became fast friends during our alternative cancer treatments in the fall of 2000.

We became fast friends during our alternative cancer treatments in the fall of 2000. Ever since then, I felt very safe and welcome with Bari Ann, almost as if she was my relative, my sister. I felt she was there for me, and I was there for her no matter what. We went through such an important time in our lives together.

I admired Bari Ann. She was very patient and smart. She really wanted to teach me, and she was a good teacher. But, as it turned out, I can remember working on the cross-stitch together only a couple of times. I stitched a small corner of the end.

In 2001, she was diagnosed again with brain cancer, and that was the end of the project. Then I did not touch it for a long time because I really did not know what to do with it. Fortunately, God sent me a friend who did know how to finish it, but it would be thirteen years before we would hang the framed piece in my living room.

Bari Ann taught me how to cross-stitch, but more importantly, she taught me about friendship and how to live life to the fullest.

I Was Pretty Busy

I met Joe in 1978 when we both lived on Prescott Avenue in Chelsea, Massachusetts. I lived in the first house on the hill, and he lived a few houses down. I was walking Derek, my youngest, in the baby carriage on a beautiful Sunday in October. David was riding his bike following us. Joe was outside cleaning his van, and we started talking.

We had a lot in common. I had been married before; he had been married before. We were both Italian, and we grew up in Chelsea. He also had two kids who lived out of state.

On that afternoon, he was telling me about his life, and I was telling him about mine. I knew some of his family; he knew some of my family. He also had a garden. I loved the fact that he grew tomatoes. He sent us home with pickled green tomatoes, and I was so impressed. He asked me if he could take us for ice cream soon, and I accepted.

Our courtship was long, but Joe and I filled it with fun surprises and interesting things to do. As we got to know each other, his family values became more and more attractive to me. Because we were very different, we lived together for a while to see how things would go. We both wanted our marriage to work.

When we met, I was definitely looking for someone who could help me raise my children. David was about eight and Derek was only about a year old. Joe missed his kids and wanted to help me raise my boys. He was a good man, and I felt safe with him. We trusted each other. I felt that this was really a good thing for all of us.

David was old enough to remember his biological father, but Joe was more or less like Derek's dad from the start. Joe was a good role model, and I enjoyed watching him father the kids. In July of 1984, Joe and I were married. We raised the kids together, and it was not easy, but it was good. It was a good decision.

In 1998, David and Alice were planning their wedding. The wedding plans took quite a bit of my time. Alice's mother was older and lived out of state—she was from Puerto Rico—so I helped Alice with all of the things that the mother of the bride normally would, like choosing her wedding gown. It was such a busy time in my life, but the wedding was beautiful; it really was. As an added benefit, when David and Alice married, I became an instant grandmother. I fell in love with Alice's daughter, Ivana; we called her Evie for short. Evie was about five or six.

At that time, I was working for a visiting nurse agency, doing home care. I also was a private nurse, and I was a massage therapist at home. Although I worked and took care of my husband

and kids, I tried to carve out time for my own hobbies and interests. I played Scrabble once a week with a friend. I liked to walk. I attended yoga classes. I always loved animals, especially dogs, and I took care of our cats, Mario and Angel—a Siamese cat and a white tabby cat. I believed in God, but I was not attending a church; I didn't know where to go and didn't have the time.

That was a time when our family was really happy together, and I wanted to enjoy the moment.

That was a time when our family was really happy together, and I wanted to enjoy the moment. When I think back, I should have made my health a priority, but I didn't; my family was my first priority.

A Glimmer of Hope

About a year earlier in 1997, I started seeing blood in my stools, and I was extremely tired. On my own, I made an appointment for a colonoscopy. It would have been my first colonoscopy, so I was a little nervous. I didn't think anything was seriously wrong; I really thought I had a hemorrhoid. At that time, I was so busy and anxious that I cancelled the appointment. There was no history of colon cancer in my family that I knew of. Maybe if there had been, I would've paid more attention. I don't know. I was a nurse, and nurses are famous for self-diagnosing and procrastinating.

It wasn't like I saw blood every time I went to the bathroom; I noticed blood every now and then. From my medical background, I knew seeing blood was not normal, but I had no pain and no other symptoms. I decided to go for a physical once David's wedding was over. My longtime primary care physician (PCP) confirmed that my red blood cell count was low. I was anemic. That was a real eye-opener.

I noticed blood every now and then.
Where was the blood coming from?

Something serious was going on. I knew I shouldn't have been anemic. *Where was the blood coming from?* In March or April—maybe even May—of 2000, I made an appointment to get the colonoscopy.

I knew that the medical community recommended a colonoscopy for women my age, but I was not happy about scheduling that appointment. I feared the procedure, but I had no idea that the prep—that diarrhea-inducing drink—would be worse than the test. I told my doctor, "This stuff should be against the law!"

I scheduled the test at a facility in Salem, Massachusetts, in June of 2000. Joe came with me. Before the colonoscopy, the doctor gave me that twilight stuff to help me relax. Now that is good stuff!

As soon as the colonoscopy was over and I was aware enough, the doctor told me he thought he found cancer. He sent a sample, a biopsy of my colon, to the pathology lab. The pathology report confirmed the cancer was rectosigmoid (stage II) cancer, a form of colorectal cancer. The doctor said I needed surgery, and I should see a surgeon *right away*.

I was devastated. I was afraid. I cried. I felt very lost. I didn't know what to do. I didn't want to tell my kids. I was worried about not being there for them. Joe did not show much emotion. He was concerned, but I felt lost even with him. I felt like I had received a death sentence.

I felt like I had received a death sentence.

When the doctor said *right away*, he meant *right away*. The doctor's office scheduled an appointment for me with a surgeon in Salem for the next day. Although Joe and I went to the appointment together and I was the patient, the surgeon never even made eye contact with me. He talked to Joe the whole time, as if I wasn't even there! It was a horrible, degrading experience.

He said, "Most likely, when I get in there, I'll have to take your appendix out. I'll probably also do a hysterectomy."

He said, "Most likely, when I get in there, I'll have to take your appendix out. I'll probably also do a hysterectomy." It was like, *Since I'm in there, I might as well take whatever I can.* I was horrified! Needless to say, when I left the office, I was absolutely a mess. All I knew was that he was not going to touch me. I said to Joe, "This is it. Get the gun." I was really in a bad way. I did not like that doctor whatsoever. I didn't know what I was going to do when I came home. It was the worst feeling I could ever imagine. I was desperate, and I was in a state of shock.

I've always felt like I had a real personal relationship with God, so I prayed a lot that night. He answered my prayer, and sent my friend Monica to help me.

That night Monica called me about a yoga class. Aside from Joe, Monica was the first person I spoke with after the Salem surgeon's appointment. I didn't even call my kids right away.

Divine Intervention

That night Monica called me about a yoga class.

I met Monica when I started taking yoga classes about six years before my diagnosis. I always loved the way she taught her students. She was a very unique and caring person. We quickly became friends.

I was very close with Monica and told her what happened in Salem. She was supportive and said everything I needed to hear. She referred me to Roger, a close friend of hers who recently battled colon cancer at a hospital in Boston. Monica was very impressed with Roger's outcome and with his surgeon. I felt as if God sent Monica to set me on the right track.

Monica and Mary, Roger's wife, knew each other from yoga class. I really trusted Monica, and she couldn't say enough about Roger and his surgeon. She said, "I'm going to give you Roger's number—Roger and Mary. Call them because I really think you should go to Boston for a second opinion. Don't go to a suburban hospital when you have something like this."

I agreed. I said, "I'm done. I'm definitely going into Boston."

So I called Roger. We ended up becoming very good friends. He gave me his surgeon's phone number so I could get a second opinion, and he told me about his whole experience.

Monica was so right. The suburban hospital was fifteen years behind the times versus Boston. I made the appointment with Roger's surgeon, Dr. B., the next day. I had the support of my husband and friends, and now I had a glimmer of hope.

Protocol

I met Dr. B. in July of 2000. Immediately, Joe and I knew he was "the man". We did not need to meet with any other surgeons. Dr. B. already had my results from the CAT scan, MRI, and colonoscopy. He knew right away that I needed surgery. He confirmed that I had rectosigmoid cancer, a form of colorectal cancer.

Then he told me exactly what he was going to do and how he was going to do it.

He sat between Joe and me in his office, held my hand, and made eye contact. Not only was he personable, but since he held a prominent position at a reputable Boston hospital, I believed he was an awesome surgeon. There was something about him. I felt like I could trust him.

He sat between Joe and me in his office, held my hand, and made eye contact.

Dr. B. said, "All I'll do is remove the cancer. We don't have to take anything else unless I find something. I'm only going to do a colorectal resection." I was so relieved! So relieved! He also said that he wanted to do it as soon as possible.

I told Dr. B. that I wanted—*needed*—to see the cancer. I'm a very visual person, and I needed to see it to believe it. He showed me the MRI and CAT scan images and pointed to the cancer. I didn't know what cancer looked like before Dr. B. shared the pictures. It looked like a big sore, like an open wound. Surprisingly, I wasn't afraid of it; the picture was merely confirmation for me. And then—I wanted to get rid of it. I definitely wanted to get it out of my body. I was afraid to have surgery, but I wanted to have it taken out as soon as possible.

We scheduled the surgery for August 1, 2000. During the time between my appointment and the surgery, I was afraid. The pictures made it look like I had cancer in only one spot, but of course, I had no idea whether the cancer had spread or not. I wouldn't know that until after the surgery. When he reviewed a preliminary CAT scan of my liver, Dr. B. discovered a couple of spots that really scared me. But luckily, he said the spots were normal, benign cysts. I was still worried that Dr. B. might find something else during the surgery.

Dr. B. removed a section of my colon and a few surrounding lymph nodes. When surgeons remove cancer, they always take lymph nodes that are around the tumor to see if the cancer has spread. Dr. B. sent my lymph nodes to the pathology department.

"Did you have to do a colostomy?"

When I was coherent, the first thing I asked was, "Did you have to do a colostomy?" A colostomy moves the collection of waste from the inside of your body to a bag outside of your body on your abdomen. I was terribly afraid of that procedure. Dr. B. told me that if the tumor had been a couple of inches lower in my colon, I would have needed a colostomy. I was extremely fortunate.

Dr. B. wanted to see me in his office for a sigmoidoscopy every three months for the first year after surgery. A sigmoidoscopy is a rectal exam with a flexible tube about a foot long. Since the surgery was so low in my colon, he could see the area that he operated on without a full colonoscopy. After a year, I would need a colonoscopy to inspect my whole colon every six months. Eventually, I would need a colonoscopy less frequently, every two to three years.

He also did a CEA blood test—a standard blood test that indicates whether cancer might be growing in your body. If the cancer had spread, that CEA number would go up. It never did. He took a blood test every time that I went in for a checkup.

While I was in the hospital recovering from the resection surgery, Dr. B. received the pathology results. He came to my room and sat by my bed to give me the news.

I anxiously asked, "What were the results?"

He answered, "We found *one* microscopic cancer cell in *one* lymph node. Years ago, we wouldn't have had the equipment and advanced technology to see this."

"What does that mean?"

"That means you need a full range of chemotherapy and radiation. That's the *standard* protocol."

I nearly died when he said that. With everything in my body—everything—I knew that I was not going that route. I knew right from that moment. I didn't know what I was going to do, but I was not going to have chemo and radiation.

> One microscopic cancer cell in one lymph node...

Then, it was like a light bulb went on. Part of me felt like asking, *Is it true?* Part of me felt like there was an underlying message. My mind repeated his words in slow motion: *One* — microscopic — cancer cell — in *one* — lymph node — that would — not be found — without this — equipment and advanced technology. The risk sounded so minute. Maybe it was me trying to format the results into my belief system. Maybe I was trying to read between the lines. I don't know; I didn't buy it. I really didn't think I needed the *standard* protocol. If they had not found the one microscopic cell, then chemotherapy and radiation would have been my personal decision.

I felt like it was done—like I had my tonsils out. I don't know what I would have done if he had said that the cancer had spread, but I knew that, with this information, I was not going to have chemo and radiation. I think we all have cancer cells in our body at one time or another, and I think our own immune system kills them. I believe we kill cancer cells many times in a lifetime because cancer is so widespread.

> *I think we all have cancer cells in our body at one time or another, and I think our own immune system kills them.*

I felt that I could cure it myself with the proper treatment, but it had to be something that was not going to hurt me. I felt the chemo and radiation was going to kill *me*, not just the cancer. I really felt that I was going to die from it. And I wasn't willing to go that route. If I was going to go, I was going naturally.

Although he knew the *standard* protocol, Dr. B. was not my oncologist. After you have surgery to remove cancer, the surgeon refers you to an oncologist, the doctor who recommends chemotherapy and radiation and follows you through your treatment. Joe and I consulted with three different oncologists in Boston.

> *I began to hate their protocol. To me, it represented fear, anger, control, and death.*

Every one of them said the same thing—the *standard* protocol is a full range of chemo and radiation! They did not deviate from their recommendation one inch. We asked, "What if Lynda only wants to have radiation and not chemotherapy, or chemotherapy and not radiation? Can't she choose?"

The answer was always, "No. It's not the *standard* protocol." They would not risk treating me unless I accepted the full course of chemotherapy and radiation. Doctors must recommend and not waver from the standard—*their*—protocol. I began to hate *their* protocol. To me, it represented fear, anger, control, and death.

The chemotherapy and radiation would have lasted at least three to six months. Since I was a nurse, I didn't even have to ask about the side effects of *their* protocol. I knew that radiation would have done a lot of damage. It probably would have affected my being able to go to the bathroom. Because it was so close to the reproductive area, it could have been the end of my sex life. I probably would have had actual burns and sores.

I believed the chemotherapy would have made me very sick—nauseous, vomiting, and exhausted. It would have destroyed my immune system. I honestly didn't think I would live through it. I knew myself. I was sensitive to and had a low tolerance for medication. I knew that was not the right way for me to go. The oncologists could not give me any guarantees. They referred to chemotherapy and radiation as prevention—to prevent the cancer from spreading. I thought, *if one microscopic cell in one lymph node was all they found, then why would I put myself through all of that?*

I reminded myself that Dr. B. already removed the cancer—the tumor and the *one* microscopic cancer cell. We were not even sure that I had cancer any longer. It hadn't metastasized somewhere; it wasn't like, *Oh my God, you have a mass. Or, the cancer has spread somewhere else.* From that point forward, I focused on my own version of prevention.

I wanted to do positive things for me. I wanted to build my immune system. I really believed that. I always tried to use natural therapies to keep myself as healthy as possible. I wanted to fight off whatever I needed to fight off with a healthy immune system.

Most people look at alternative treatments as risky. Not me. I honestly looked at the chemo and radiation like it was going to kill *me*, not the cancer itself. I knew without question that if I did chemo and radiation, that was my death sentence. I knew it. I had so much faith—in my decisions, my professional medical experience, my knowledge of myself—I was going to take care of this with alternative treatments. I was going to build up my immune system, my whole system, my whole constitution. I was going to get healthy, health*ier*.

Most people look at alternative treatments as risky. Not me.

After I made my decision, I was really nervous because I didn't know how my husband and my kids and everyone would feel when they learned I had refused chemo and radiation. But the people who were most important in my life—my kids, my husband—were absolutely one hundred percent supportive. I was so surprised that they respected my wishes.

I was much more afraid of the traditional treatment than I was of the cancer. People didn't understand that. Most of them said, "Oh my God, you're so brave. I can't believe you're doing this. How can you take this chance? Aren't you afraid?" I would say, "Brave?" I didn't feel like I was brave. I knew what they meant, but I was looking at it from a totally different perspective. I couldn't—just *couldn't* do it. I never felt that I made the wrong choice. The *standard* protocol might be the right choice for some patients, but I was adamantly against chemotherapy and radiation for myself. There was not one question. I went to those oncologists to appease my family and my

I prayed very hard through the whole ordeal, and asked God for guidance...

husband—for curiosity, I guess—but I decided that was not the route for me.

I prayed very hard through the whole ordeal, and asked God for guidance because I didn't know where I was going to go or what I was going to do. I surrounded myself with people who came from a holistic background and were in agreement with me—people who were supportive. But there definitely were other people who tried to talk me out of it.

For example, Roger, Monica's friend who recommended Dr. B., tried to talk me out of it. By that time, he and Mary were very good friends of mine as well. He was from the other belief system, though, and he fought his cancer using chemo and radiation. He thought if he introduced me to some cancer patients, he could convince me to follow his lead. He volunteered on the chemo floor of another Boston hospital, and asked me to go with him to meet his chemo center friends. To appease him, I said, "Okay. I'll go with you." While we drove to the hospital together, he tried to sell me on the *standard* protocol. He was afraid I was making the wrong decision, and he really cared about me.

We walked up to the treatment room. The whole floor was filled with people in recliners—recliner after recliner after recliner—receiving chemotherapy intravenously. We didn't visit with everyone, but Roger saw lots of patients while they were receiving chemo. I talked to a few people and told them about my diagnosis. It was an informative experience for me. Although I didn't mind going in and talking with the people, I had no intention—absolutely no intention—of receiving chemo. I went because I felt that Roger really wanted me to go. Seeing people receiving chemo, though, made me feel even stronger and more confident about my decision.

This period was a scary and painful part of my life, but I grew as a person. For the first time, I truly owned my health. Although perhaps unpopular choices, I rejected impersonal doctors and standard treatments. I found supportive doctors, chose to cure myself with a healthy immune system, and intended to do everything I could that was positive. I didn't know my plan yet, but I knew I would choose to follow *my* protocol.

> *For the first time, I truly owned my health.*

I Believe in Miracles

As I was leaving with Roger, we had to walk through another section of the chemo floor where people were receiving intravenous. I happened to look over, and my good friend Anne was in a recliner. We hadn't seen each other in—it had to be—at least 10 years. She had been my instructor in massage school as well as my massage therapist.

We noticed each other, and she practically jumped off the chair. We were hugging, and she said, "Oh my God, Lynda, I haven't seen you in so

Divine Intervention

I happened to look over, and my good friend Anne was in a recliner.

long. What are you doing here?" I said the same to her, "What are *you* doing here?"

Since massage school is an intimate type of situation, she got to know me very well, and I respected her. One day Anne said to me, "Lynda, I think you would really benefit from a 12-step program like Al-Anon." I must have told her my history, but she also could probably tell from my personality that I needed something like a 12-step program. She had been through one, and she could see that I needed it. My father was an alcoholic, and my first husband, Phil, came home from Vietnam addicted to drugs. So I had been around a lot of addiction in my life. Thank God I didn't have the problem, but I was affected by the disease.

I was so angry when she said she thought I needed a 12-step program. But I wasn't looking at it the right way. I was looking at it like, *Are you kidding me? I have to go do something like* that *because of* them? I wasn't realizing that I had certain characteristics—that Al-Anon was not for *them*, it was for *me*. I had it all wrong. I was so mad; I could have hit her that day! She really hit a nerve. When I looked into it though, I understood. Al-Anon was not for *them*. Al-Anon was to help *me*. Then I was all for it, and it was one of the best things that I could have done for myself. Moments like the Al-Anon discussion helped Anne and me become very close friends. I respected her and loved her dearly; she could always see right through me.

On that day in August of 2000, I took our chance meeting as another sign. She was at the hospital receiving a medication called Herceptin to prevent a recurrence of breast cancer. Herceptin decreases the estrogen in your body and is not harmful to your body. When I told her about my situation, she said, "Oh my God! I really, really want to tell you about Dr. Keller. I went to see him in Ireland. He uses Carnivora treatments. Please call me. Call me tonight."

She gave me her number, and I called her that night. Anne told me Dr. Helmut Keller focused on improving the immune system. She recommended a book called *Choices*, by Marion Morra and Eve

Potts, which explained Dr. Keller's Carnivora treatments. At that time, I didn't know anything about Carnivora except what Anne told me—that Carnivora is a supplement derived from the Venus flytrap plant. She gave me all the information to reach Dr. Keller in Ireland at his clinic, and that's where it all began.

The talk with Anne and the Choices *book made me realize that I could select from an awful lot of alternatives.*

The talk with Anne and the *Choices* book made me realize that I could select from an awful lot of alternatives. I felt so strongly about Dr. Keller because of Anne and the way everything transpired. I could see the divine intervention from person to person to person to person. It all felt right. I can't say how I knew, but I knew in my heart that it was the right choice.

I called Dr. Keller and spoke with him for a while on the phone. Although he practiced at the East Clinic in Ireland, he was German and had a thick accent. He sounded very caring and professional. I couldn't wait to go, and I couldn't wait to meet him. Of course, I was definitely nervous and going all the way to Europe was a little scary, but I felt that it was right.

Dr. Keller asked me to write a letter explaining everything, including all of my medical records. He would use the information to determine how much time I would need in Ireland and to determine the right treatment regimen for me. By the end of the phone call, we knew that I was a good candidate for his treatments. Soon, I would be going to Ireland.

After the major surgery, I had to heal and get stronger. Dr. Keller wanted me to come to Ireland in October, two and half months after my surgery. He originally thought that I would stay there for two weeks. That was before he saw me, gave me a physical, and saw how I responded to treatment. In the end, I was only there for one week of treatment.

Before my trip to Ireland, I was so excited that I told my yoga class about Dr. Keller and the Carnivora treatment. While we were changing into our yoga clothes one day, I was chatting with my friend Valerie. "I'm going to Ireland for treatments with Dr. Keller."

Valerie was shocked, "Oh my God! I have a friend in Newton. Her name is Bari Ann, and I think she is going to Ireland for that treatment. It

Divine
Intervention

"Oh my God! I have a friend in Newton. Her name is Bari Ann, and I think she is going to Ireland for that treatment."

sounds like you are going to see the same doctor at the same clinic."

I couldn't believe it. So right away she said, "I'm going to hook you up with Bari Ann. Talk to her. Maybe you guys are doing the same thing."

Valerie owned a natural food store, and I worked there for a short time. She was very knowledgeable and had a calm and caring nature. Because they were in a philosophy group together, Valerie and Bari Ann knew each other very well. I followed up on Valerie's recommendation and called Bari Ann. Later, I found out that Bari Ann was also a friend of Anne's; they lived close by to each other, and we were all massage therapists. It was amazing, just amazing—another link—everybody was all connected.

Everything unfolded as if somebody—God— was guiding me. He put all the people I needed in all the right places so I could have my own treatment plan, *my* protocol. What were the chances really? I don't think people believed it. *I* could hardly believe it. It felt like a miracle, and I do believe in miracles.

It Was Like a Vacation

Bari Ann and I talked on the phone that night. She confirmed that we were going to Ireland at the same time to see the same doctor. We met the next day. It was the end of September already.

Bari Ann had breast cancer then uterine cancer. She had already tried radiation and chemotherapy, and she didn't want any more. She was a very holistic and positive person. She decided that she would try Dr. Keller's Carnivora treatments. Dr. Keller scheduled Bari Ann for two weeks of treatment. We connected right away and became very close.

Even though Bari Ann and I were going for treatment at the same time, I didn't feel like our medical history was similar enough to compare our experiences. I felt like my case was so minute that I was trying to prevent the cancer from coming back. I felt like I had the chicken pox virus, and it went away—done. I was going to Ireland right after surgery, and I was feeling great.

I didn't feel like our medical history was similar enough to compare our experiences.

On the other hand, when she went to Ireland, Bari Ann was not feeling well. Bari Ann was trying to build herself back up to prevent cancer, as I was, but her immune system was already damaged from the chemo and radiation. Dr. Keller had a higher success rate with patients who had not compromised their immune systems.

Of course, my insurance didn't cover Dr. Keller's treatments or our travel to Ireland, but even the out-of-pocket costs had to be cheaper than traditional chemotherapy and radiation. Bari Ann and her mother, Selma, left for Ireland during the first week of October in 2000, and Joe and I joined them a week later.

We flew out of Logan Airport into the Shannon Airport, County Clare, Ireland, and we took a cab from the airport to the Tinarana House in Killaloe, County Clare. Our cab driver immediately knew how to get to the clinic. He was awesome, super friendly, and couldn't do enough for us. We felt like we had known him all of our lives.

Patients came from all over the world to see Dr. Keller. The Tinarana House, which was attached to the East Clinic, was a place for his patients and their families to stay. The close proximity of our lodging and the clinic allowed the staff to control our diet and check on us any time of the day or night. Everybody we met in Ireland was so friendly. They were the warmest people I've ever met. I felt so cared for by everyone at the clinic and the Tinarana House. I've traveled many places, and the Irish are the nicest people I've ever met.

When we arrived, we met the Tinarana House staff. We ate dinner with Bari Ann and Selma. Dr.

Keller was there too—it was common for him to eat dinner with his patients. After dinner, he explained that we would start with a physical and blood work at the clinic in the morning.

Dr. Keller was in his late sixties. He was a big man, who made me feel like he would take me under his wing and protect me. I felt so safe with him, almost like he was the father figure I never had. I lived in fear of my own father as he passed me from relative to relative during alcoholic episodes. Dr. Keller was the opposite of my father. He was like a friend—like family. Even though he was married, Dr. Keller spent a lot of time at the clinic and the Tinarana House following the progress of his patients. Dr. Keller was grooming his associate Dr. Santa Cruz to take over the practice when Dr. Keller wanted to retire. Dr. Santa Cruz also treated Bari Ann and me.

After the initial evaluation in the morning, Dr. Keller recommended intravenous Carnivora, hyperthermia, a nutritious diet, supplements, liquid Carnivora, and Carnivora in pill form. Carnivora is

I felt so safe with him, almost like he was the father figure I never had.

natural and chemical-free. A long time ago, Dr. Keller realized that the Venus flytrap plant was able to distinguish between healthy cells and unhealthy cells. The following is an excerpt from a letter he sent to me explained his findings:

Letter from Dr. Keller

In 1973, more than thirty years ago, I discovered why Carnivora is such an effective dietary supplement for the immune system. As you know, this plant is an expert at trapping its own meals through a sensitive biological response process. When a fly or other small insect touches the delicate hairs of the plant's "mouth," it causes the mouth to close quickly, trapping the insect inside the plant. The juicy liquids inside the plant's mouth are capable of digesting animal and vegetable materials. Interestingly, they do not, however, digest the plant itself. From this observation, I concluded that the Venus flytrap plant must have an advanced immune system capable of distinguishing between harmful intruder organisms and its own materials.

Even though I knew this treatment was the right decision, I anxiously waited to see if I would experience an adverse reaction. I wasn't used to putting something in my bloodstream. Dr. Keller told me there were no negative side effects and I believed him, but a little part of me still wanted to see how I would respond.

The East Clinic looked like a regular clinic with offices and exam rooms, but one thing was different from the Boston hospital—no *rows* of recliners. Bari Ann and I did receive our treatments while sitting in recliners, but it was a more intimate setting than I saw when I visited the cancer ward with Roger. The clinic was basic and small, but very friendly. The nurses were always right there with us.

Bari Ann and I received intravenous Carnivora treatments twice a day for about an hour each time. We sat in recliners and talked and talked—it felt like we knew each other forever. Through those conversations, we learned we had a lot in common. We were the same age, were married and had children. We each led holistic lives—we were massage therapists, practiced yoga and ate organic food.

We were not exactly the same, however. Bari Ann was a vegetarian, but I was not. One night when we were in Ireland, she ate a piece of meat after one of her treatments. I think she was still feeling a little woozy from the medication, relaxed. It was so funny because she really liked it. When she ate it, we laughed. It was as if she did not have a care in the world! I think it took until the next day before she realized that she actually ate a piece of steak.

We ate breakfast and dinner with Joe and Selma at the Tinarana House, but we spent almost all of our day at the clinic. Bari Ann and her husband, Marty, spoke on the phone every day; he was very supportive, and they were very close. Bari Ann and Selma were going through some mother-daughter problems. She and her mother were very close, but they went kind of toe-to-toe sometimes. They had their differences, but I think I helped them become closer. I think I was able to help in that respect, simply by listening to Bari Ann. She asked my opinion about certain things, and I gave her some insight. Usually I ended with, "How important is this really, Bari Ann? Let it go." I guess I was able to draw on all my years of therapy, Al-Anon, and tough love.

We had a little free time, but not much. While we received the Carnivora treatments, Joe and Selma spent their free time getting to know each other. Bari Ann's mother was a wonderful lady. They did a little bit of sightseeing, and we joined them once or twice. It was nice to be outdoors; it was a beautiful place.

Joe didn't join me for my intravenous treatments, but he was present for and observed the whole hyperthermia treatment. People are always surprised when I tell them I used hyperthermia to fight cancer. Here's how I think of it: Cancer cells are new and growing. That means they are unstable and easy to detect. They definitely do not like heat. Even traditional, mainstream doctors use hyperthermia along with other cancer treatments because heat can kill or damage cancer cells. Hyperthermia works similarly to our bodies when we have an infection; our bodies auto-matically produce a fever. The treatment damages

People are always surprised when I tell them I used hyperthermia to fight cancer.

the cells, and then the Carnivora detects and attacks the abnormal, unstable, potentially cancerous cells.

Joe came with me to the hyperthermia treatment because I was really nervous; it was scary. The nurses gave me a sedative to put me in a twilight sleep. I could hear the doctors—they never leave you during the hyperthermia treatment—but I was kind of in a light sleep. Nothing hurt at all; there was no pain. When the doctors were ready, infrared lights were used to slowly increase my whole body temperature. I don't know what the exact temperature was, but it could have reached between 105 and 109 degrees Fahrenheit. I was hooked up to all kinds of monitors, and it was very warm. It took about an hour, and then I had the Carnivora intravenous treatment.

As part of *my* protocol, Dr. Keller instructed me to eat lots of yellow vegetables and fruit—squash, peppers, pineapple, cantaloupe, anything in the yellow family. Everything had to be organic. I was to eat organic red meat once a week. He didn't believe people should be total vegetarians. He recommended that everyone, even vegetarians, eat organic, red meat at least once a week. I could also eat fish. He told me to drink pineapple juice, Chinese tea, Essiac tea, and lots of water. But I was definitely not allowed to eat sugar. Cancer cells love sugar, so he wanted me totally off sugar.

We were staying in this beautiful home in Ireland and eating awesome food. I had a great appetite. I didn't have any negative side effects from my treatments; I felt great. It was really like a vacation because I felt so good. There was nothing bad about it at all.

When my treatments in Ireland were complete, Dr. Keller sent me home with a six-month supply of Carnivora liquid injections and a letter explaining why I needed the supplements. Although Carnivora in pill form was legal in the United States, liquid Carnivora was not. I thought it was worth the risk to continue my treatment, and Dr. Keller thought a note might help if anyone questioned me. Every day for six months, I gave myself an injection, and luckily, no one ever found out. After that, I took the pills for another six months.

I also received follow-up treatments at an alternative health center in Cambridge, Massachusetts. The health center was a perfect mix of

Eastern and Western medicine, alternative and traditional. I received regular checkups every six months.

At the health center, I saw an acupuncturist who specialized in cancer prevention. I also received vitamin C intravenously to boost my immune system.

Divine Intervention

I met Nancy at the health center, and we became friends.

I started to study homeopathy myself—I think it is wonderful medicine—and I took some cancer prevention remedies. I met Nancy at the health center, and we became friends. She was a nurse and the manager of the IV clinic. I saw her there a lot, and since I loved the center's mission, I wanted to work there. Eventually, I asked Nancy if the center needed any nurses, and they did. By January of 2001, I was working with Nancy as my supervisor. I'm so glad I met her; she eventually saved my life.

My time in Ireland and at the health center in Cambridge was not only about alternative cancer fighting therapies. The friendship, love and support that I felt at the Tinarana House, the East Clinic, and the health center proved to be essential components of *my* protocol.

Left to Right: Dr. Santa Cruz, Lynda, Bari Ann,
Dr. Keller, Selma, Joe

Dr. Keller always
encouraged
Bari Ann and me!
Here he is hugging
us goodbye after we
completed our
treatments.

The Tinarana House, our home away from home
during our Carnivora treatments

The Tinarana House dining room

Flying High

After I got back from Ireland, I felt like I was flying high. I felt so much love. I felt like I could do anything. It was amazing. I had no fear, no fear at all. I was empowered—maybe for the first time in my life. I had made my own decisions, and I was sure they were the right decisions.

I don't know if it was the treatments or the supplements that made me look so healthy, but people would say, "Wow! You look awesome." They were expecting me to look sick—my surgery was only two-and-a-half months earlier—and they were surprised that I looked so good.

Unfortunately, my "high" didn't last forever. It's almost like when you're a newlywed or recently gave birth to a baby—when you have a big life-changing event—you are euphoric for a little while. I felt like I could do anything. It was a very freeing feeling.

As I came down from my high in early April of 2001, I started to feel disconnected and a little depressed. I turned to my father figure, Dr. Keller. I wrote him an email with medical and personal updates plus questions about my ongoing supplements. I ended the email with the following:

> I need my endorphins and I don't want to have a reoccurrence of cancer. Please help me to have a better attitude! I know that I can do it.

> With much love and gratitude,

> Lynda

Dr. Keller was on vacation with his wife, but when he returned, he came through as expected. He wrote:

> Well it's a pleasure to hear that your cancer gave up for the moment and you had your 50th birthday celebration—my congratulations—you are not bound to your profession anymore, you have problems with money, and everybody is healthy. This all sounds like life as it is. Everything is in disorder—namely in balance.... Live like a maniac, enjoy sex with your husband... talk about the damned money after pleasure. You are free for the future, and if something comes up, we can handle it. Who knows what is going to happen to both of us. Let's enjoy life as it is in the moment and don't bother about the next 50 years.
>
> Sincerely yours, Dr. H. Keller

Beating cancer gave me insight, courage, and confidence. It made me realize that life is short, and that it was time to do some things on my bucket list. I traveled. I went to Italy about four times to visit my son Derek. I went on a Western Caribbean cruise. I went to Niagara Falls and Florida. I did anything that I really wanted to do, within reason of course.

I made more life-changing decisions too. I realized I didn't want to be tied to a job so I started working on my own as a self-employed nurse. My boys were grown, which left Joe and me with the house to ourselves. I started thinking about whether my marriage was everything I wanted it to be. It took a while, but Joe and I finally decided to divorce in 2007. Those were both big steps.

I was finally living my life authentically.

During this post-cancer season of my life, I didn't really think about the cancer. I lived without fear, and I took risks. I was finally living my life authentically.

Two Butterflies

In March of 2001, about five months after our treatment, Bari Ann bought the cross-stitch project for me. She chose a beautiful Asian fan with flowers and a large butterfly right in the center. The fan had a light green background, and the flowers were bright shades of blue and pink. Gold accents made the fan look rich and regal.

We chose to spend so much time together with intravenous needles and tubes, and now we chose to spend time together with needles and thread. There were lots of crosses left to fill on that fabric, but we were hopeful that we could finish it together.

It meant a lot to me that Bari Ann would spend precious time teaching me how to cross-stitch. We had been through a lot

Two butterflies had transformed from cancer patients to sisters.

together. There had been times when one of us would get frightened or depressed, but we were able to share those experiences with each other. We were really there for each other, and we knew when it got tough, we would pick each other up again.

When I focused on the butterfly, it reminded me of the freedom and peace we both felt at that moment. It reminded me of how much our friendship had grown. We—two butterflies—had transformed from cancer patients to sisters.

That freeing feeling diminished the following month. In late April of 2001, Bari Ann's doctors told her she had brain cancer.

As we cross-stitched, I was hoping that Bari Ann was not going to get sick again. She really did well after Ireland for the first six months. She felt the best she had ever felt.

Everyone, even her surgeon, thought she was cured of everything. She felt terrific, and she looked wonderful. She had energy. She was back to her old self. She thought she was totally out of the woods. Then she started falling. Her doctors determined that she had a brain tumor. She had more surgery, but the procedure didn't eliminate all of the brain cancer, and it eventually spread.

I was devastated when she told me, heart-broken. I spent as much time with Bari Ann as I could. I visited with her. I helped her shower and cook meals. I gave her massages to ease her pain. And of course, we talked. We shared. We hung out. We were really, really close, and we both knew that time together was short—a gift.

She never called me in the middle of the night, but she knew she could. We knew that if I was having a bad day or she was having a bad day, we would drop everything to be together—to be there for each other and lift each other up.

Bari Ann always had a positive attitude. She was the type that wasn't going to give in, wasn't going to give up—she was going to do everything she could. Even when she was sick, she still had hope, and she fought like crazy. She fought for her kids, her husband, and our friendship until she couldn't do it anymore.

Some people go into hospice and die at home. Bari Ann was getting her care at home for a long time, but at the very end, she was in the hospital. On April 28, 2003, her husband, Marty, called and told me she died in the hospital. We were lucky to have enjoyed two more years together.

Hospice

After my surgery, I had three girlfriends who had cancer at the same time. They were all close friends of mine: Bari Ann, Maureen, and Jocelyn. Maureen was a good friend I knew from nursing. Jocelyn was a sculptor and a teacher who had lots of pieces in the deCordova Museum in Lexington, Massachusetts. We all had cancer together, and I lost every one of them within one year. I was with each of them as they died. After that, I knew that I was called to work with hospice patients. I started working as a hospice nurse in 2006.

At first, I was afraid of focusing on hospice. Although I wanted to help and I felt like it was my calling, I didn't know if I could do it. I didn't know if I had the skills or the qualities, but I really wanted to try. I learned that I was a very good hospice nurse. Hospice is different from taking care of the elderly. Every day I saw about six people who were at the end of their life. Other than pain medication and routine medical care, the biggest thing hospice patients want is for someone to be present. I was able to be present with each patient, because I was kind of there myself at one point. Caring for my patients wasn't scary to me. In fact, I really wanted to be with these people until the end.

At first, I was afraid of focusing on hospice.

Dame Cicely Saunders founded the modern hospice movement. I love this quote from her biographer, Shirley du Boulay, "The dying need the friendship of the heart—its qualities of care, acceptance, vulnerability; but they also need the skills of the mind—the most sophisticated treatment that medicine has to offer. On its own, neither is enough."[i] That quote spoke volumes to me. I really felt that God called me to hospice work.

I never told any of my patients my story. I was a professional, and they had already made their own decisions. The damage was already done. So instead of sharing my story, I shared my compassion. Some nurses can't do hospice because they think it is too depressing or they can't bear to watch people suffer. They think it's so sad. But I didn't look at it that way; I looked at it like, *I'm going to give this person the absolute best quality of life in their last days that they could possibly have.*

All of the people I took care of during that season of my nursing career either died or were in the process of dying while on chemo or radiation. They suffered so many negative side effects from their treatments. The whole experience was reassurance that I had made the right choice for myself.

The Reindeer on the Couch

Eventually, my life became routine again. I still felt healthy, but I cheated on my diet every once in a while. I had made changes in my life, and I lived life with slightly more passion than some of my friends.

I was living by myself in Wakefield, Massachusetts in 2012 in a rented, two-bedroom apartment, the upstairs of a two-family home. It was plenty of room for me, and it was all mine. I could decorate as I chose. I could visit with friends when I wanted. Aside from the occasional commuter train that passed by my backyard, I enjoyed the freedom of solitude. But living alone also had its drawbacks, and I felt one of those drawbacks early one morning.

I woke up about two or three in the morning with severe—and I mean severe—abdominal pain. Initially I thought it might be food poisoning. The terrible pain in my stomach was unbearable, and the vomiting was not normal. I knew something was seriously wrong; it wasn't simply a stomach bug. We all experience pain, but this pain was unlike any pain I've ever felt; I was doubled-over. I waited about an hour, but it kept getting worse. So that's when I decided to call my friend Nancy. Maybe I should have called 911, but I didn't. I called Nancy.

Nancy and her husband, Ethan, arrived around 4:30 in the morning. Nancy used to work in trauma and the emergency room, so she had a lot of relevant experience. After about another hour, they said that they were taking me to the hospital because I wasn't getting any better; I was still vomiting and doubled-over, but I didn't want to go.

So they said, "We'll see if you can drink something," but I couldn't; I couldn't keep anything down. Finally, they said, "That's it. We're taking you to the hospital."

Although they did not take me to the same hospital that admitted me in 2000, it was a good thing that Nancy and Ethan took me to a *Boston* hospital. Four hours later, Dr. B. was performing major surgery. The very same doctor who performed the colorectal section twelve years prior was on duty at a second Boston facility. What were the odds?

Divine Intervention

Four hours later, Dr. B. was performing major surgery.

The emergency room doctors did a CAT scan, and they saw a blockage. A blockage is very dangerous. If you have a blockage in your bowel, your intestines, it can become necrotic—the blood supply can be cut off. It's definitely life-threatening, and that's why I had emergency surgery. It was pretty shocking. One day I was fine, and the next day, I was recovering from major surgery.

Since he knew my history, Dr. B. was able to reopen my original incision from the colon cancer. The surgery to remove the cancer, as bad as it was, was planned; I knew I was going in for surgery. But this was like a shock to everything, a blow to my whole system—mentally, emotionally, physically—because it was not planned.

When I woke up from surgery, I had no idea where I was for about four days. I was in a state of shock. I'd wake up in pain and look around. They had trouble finding the right pain medication because I'm so sensitive. My mind was in and out, sleeping and waking up. It was a good thing that my son David and my friend Nancy were there, because I was hallucinating from the medication. It was awful.

My son Derek was living in Italy during that time. David and Derek were on the phone every day trying to decide whether Derek should come home or not. Of course, I wanted him with me, but I knew it would be hard for him to come home and then get back to his life in Italy. So I was okay with his decision not to come.

Everyone scars differently after surgery. Scar tissue grows, and when it gets stuck and heals in place, that's called an adhesion. Scar tissue, fascia, is very strong, but very thin; it's almost like cellophane in a way. I had one big adhesion that was causing the blockage and lots of small adhesions throughout my small intestines. I asked Dr. B. what it looked like. He told me the adhesions caused my small intestines to twist like a braid, so he had to cut and release the fascia. I basically got a full cleaning with that surgery. Unfortunately, there is no way to monitor adhesions, so it could happen again without warning.

I was in the hospital for eight days. I guess I started to "come to" after the fourth day. The first thing I asked was, "Do I have a colostomy?" I figured the cancer was back; I didn't even think about a blockage. Thank God, I did not need a colostomy. I think Dr. B. was pleased that he was able to go in and remove all of the adhesions at one time. It definitely gave me peace to know that a surgeon I trusted was in there and could confirm that the cancer was gone.

Boy, it took a long time for me to heal, though. With the cancer removal, they went in, and they knew exactly what they planned to do.

They only did the resection and sewed me up. With the adhesion surgery, Dr. B. had to do a lot of cutting. He had to cut me further up and remove all the adhesions because they were not all in one spot. When they told me I was ready to go home, I wasn't even thinking that far ahead. I didn't think, *How am I going to get up the stairs, and who is going to take care of me?*

I mentioned to Nancy, "Gee, they're going to send me home."

"You're not going home. You're coming to stay with us."

Still surprised, I asked "What do you mean?"

"You can't go home right now. You need someone to take care of you. You can't go up the stairs, and you shouldn't be by yourself." I probably would've had to go to a rehab facility, if I didn't have Nancy and Ethan.

Even though I was recovering when I stayed at Nancy and Ethan's house, it was awesome, just awesome. It was around Christmastime. Christmas, for them, is a very big deal, and they do a ton of decorating. I couldn't do much, because I was still in a lot of pain. I couldn't even go up their stairs, so I stayed on the couch. I would take a nap, and then all a sudden, I would open my eyes and the Christmas tree was up! Then I would go to sleep again, and when I woke up, the whole room was like a winter wonderland. One time I started crying. It really touched me. It was unbeliev-able. Every day it got better

All a sudden I would open my eyes and the Christmas tree was up!

and better. Honestly. They got a big kick out of it. They were calling me the "reindeer on the couch".

Nancy's son came home for Christmas. On Christmas Day, David and Evie came over. David loves to cook, so he fit right in and helped prepare the meal. Aside from missing Derek, having our two families together for Christmas was perfect. The whole recovery was amazing.

There is Always a Meaning Behind It—Always

After Bari Ann got sick, I put that butterfly cross-stitch back in its cocoon in a drawer. Every once in a while, I would think about it, and I'd want to finish it because it was so special to me. It wasn't until March of 2013, twelve years later, that it was resurrected from the depths of my cancer memories. So much had happened since then. Bari

Ann died; Joe and I divorced; I cared for lots of cancer patients; I had the adhesion surgery; and Nancy and I became even closer friends, like sisters.

Nancy is very creative and good with her hands. I saw her doing a project one day when I was at her house, and it reminded me of the fan. I asked her if she would teach me someday. I told her that I wanted to bring the fan to her house and maybe she could help me start again and continue. So I found it in the drawer and brought it over to her house.

Nancy's house is very warm, comfy, and cozy. Even before I was the reindeer on the couch, I felt like her place was my home away from home. Of course, she agreed to teach me, but it wasn't quite the same as learning from Bari Ann. Nancy is a perfectionist, and I am not. Since Nancy is right-handed and I am left-handed, learning the motions was a little awkward and complicated. But I thought I had it, so I came home and planned to work on it once in a while. I finished a little bit more of the corner, but not much.

One day Nancy said to bring the cross-stitch over so I could show her how much I had done. How can I say it? It was *unique* because I did it, and I wasn't doing it perfectly. Ethan kept saying, "Why don't you let Lynda do it the way she wants to do it, and see how it comes out?"

I thought about his suggestion, but it was such a beautiful piece, and it was so important to me, that I wanted it done correctly. Nancy asked if I wanted her to finish it for me, and I finally said, "Okay."

I gave it to her and then forgot about it again. She had a very busy life, and I didn't know when she would have time to work on it, so I figured she'd finish it someday. I didn't want to ask her about it and add any pressure. I hadn't touched it in twelve years; I wasn't in a hurry.

Nancy and I did not see each other on Christmas Day of 2013. We had our own little Christmas at her house when she got back. She absolutely loved to do special things. She wouldn't give you a gift purely to give you a gift. There was always a meaning behind it—always.

She wrapped her gifts beautifully with a personal card. Nancy loved to send cards. She was the only person I knew who sent cards for every occasion, and I loved to receive them. I've always thought that it's so special to get a handwritten card in the mail.

She also loved to surprise, and she certainly did surprise me that day. As I peeled back the beautiful Christmas paper and unstuck the frilly bow, I carefully opened the box and realized that she had given me the most special gift of all. There in front of me were gorgeous flowers that leapt off the fabric and one lone butterfly—free and complete.

There in front of me were gorgeous flowers that leapt off the fabric and one lone butterfly— free and complete.

We spent another wonderful day going to the store to pick out the frame together. Whenever we get together, we make a day of it. We have fun. We play. We live life to the fullest.

Nancy knew how much finishing that project meant to me. I hammered the nail into the wall, and together we hung the special artwork for all to see.

My Protocol

Fourteen years after my cancer diagnosis, I still take good care of myself, but I can see my age. I can see it in my body. I can see it in my face. I feel like I'm pretty active; I don't feel like I'm slowing down. Maybe I am, but I don't notice it. I'm surprised when people tell me I don't look my age, because I feel like I do.

I'm really careful about what I eat, but I'm not as strict as I was. I don't follow Dr. Keller's dietary advice one hundred percent, but I am very vigilant. I still go to yoga, and do whatever type of bodywork I feel is right at the time. When I was first diagnosed, I didn't want massage, but I did see other types of bodywork practitioners. For instance, my friend Karen is an expert in myofascial release. Fascia is so strong and so pervasive throughout your body, including all of your muscles and organs, that when it gets stuck, you can have lots of problems. It's almost like you are Spider-Man. Karen helps break up that fascia so you have fewer problems, and I felt like I needed that treatment right after my diagnosis.

I've also looked into a place called Clear Passage Physical Therapy in Florida. They invented and practice the Wurn Technique to remove adhesions from the small bowel, colon and other parts of the body. All of the practitioners are highly trained physical therapists. It's pretty impressive. Their technique uses manipulation, like physical therapy manipulation, to remove the adhesions—or unstick them. I like the technique; it's like massage in a sense but much more specific. It's really an alternative to surgery for people who catch the adhesions when they are still mild, before it's a life-threatening emergency. So that is a place that I would like to visit and explore. That adhesion surgery was so debilitating—so much worse than the cancer surgery—that I would do anything to prevent adhesions in the future. When I feel something's right, I feel it in my gut. I really know when it's right for me to do something. I've always been that way, and this set of cancer experiences caused me to trust my intuition even more. My intuition is guiding the way I feel about the colonoscopy I'm supposed to schedule this year. I don't feel like it's the

When I feel something's right, I feel it in my gut.

right time. I'm not saying I will never go for another colonoscopy, but I don't feel like it's the right time right now. I read about a new noninvasive colonoscopy option. When that procedure is available, then maybe I'll consider it'. But right now, I don't want to put my body through that whole procedure.

I really listen to my body. It's obvious from my cancer treatments, I don't automatically do everything that traditional doctors recommend. For example, I've only had one mammogram in my whole life—years ago. I was starting menopause, and I started to feel some hard breast tissue on the sides of my breasts. I thought, *What the hell is this?* So my doctor sent me for a mammogram. After the mammogram, the doctor said, "Oh you have fibrocystic breast tissue, and we want to take a biopsy." I said, "No. No biopsy. You're not doing a biopsy on me." Every woman gets fibrocystic breast tissue when she gets older. Doctors do these mammograms and they find *problems* like fibrocystic breast tissue and cancer cells. Before you know it, you're having your breast removed, going through chemo, and dying. I don't believe in it. I massaged my breasts, and the hard tissue went away. I also think caffeine had a lot to do with it, so I gave up coffee. I think many people have had breast cancer, and their immune systems cured the cancer without further medical treatment.

Numerous doctors have asked me to go for mammograms over the years, but they all have to say that I refused. People ask me, "Are you crazy? You are a nurse. How could you not go for mammograms? What's wrong with you?" I had one. That is all I needed. I do self-exams. Every time I go for a physical, the doctor does a breast exam. I am not putting myself through that. I do not believe in getting a biopsy. It is very invasive to me, and I think it causes more problems. Again, it is *their* protocol.

I do not follow the Carnivora therapies anymore. I know Dr. Keller retired but still sells Carnivora online. Dr. Santa Cruz moved back to Tijuana, Mexico, but I don't think he administers Carnivora treatments any longer. I look at Carnivora as a supplement that enhances your immune system, and it's not only for cancer cells; it can cure many different ailments. I wish more people knew about it, used it, and were not afraid of it. In my opinion, I think they should be afraid of the other stuff, the chemo and radiation. So whenever people ask me to tell my story about my treatments, I tell them—but I also remind them that *they must make their own decisions.*

Eastern and Western medicine offer lots of treatment options, and I think patients should

Eastern and Western medicine offer lots of treatment options, and I think patients should explore all of them.

explore all of them. Find out what traditional medicine recommends—*their* protocol. Find out what the side effects of *their* protocol could be. Then look into other alternative treatments. People need to educate themselves. Find out all the information that they possibly can, and then follow the path that they feel is right for themselves.

I try to live a good lifestyle and keep my immune system as healthy as possible. I try to have a spiritual outlook on life. I spend time with supportive family and friends. That's my protocol.

People ask me if I am afraid that the cancer will come back because I did not follow *their* protocol. There's always a chance that the colon cancer could come back. Always. Anyone can get cancer at any time. I could get cancer again, and it might not have anything to do with the colon cancer. Nobody's immune to it. But on a daily basis, I don't think about cancer. If the cancer came back, I probably would be afraid, but I do not expect it to come back. I feel like I had my tonsils out, and they're gone. I take care of myself. I try to live a good lifestyle and keep my immune system as healthy as possible. I try to have a spiritual outlook on life. I spend time with supportive family and friends. That's *my* protocol.

I pray to God to show me the good in my life and to guide me. I have a lot of faith now, and I had a lot of faith when I was going through cancer and treatment. I think everybody has an inner guidance that they shouldn't be afraid of and they should really listen to. That's our divine connection. We need to look for it; we need to be present to acknowledge it.

If Monica hadn't called me the night I had my first colonoscopy, then she would not have recommended that I speak to Roger. If I hadn't met Roger, I never would have been on the chemo floor and run into Anne. If I hadn't seen Anne, I would not have heard about Dr. Keller. If I hadn't talked to Valerie about the Carnivora treatments, I would not have met Bari Ann. If I hadn't scheduled my follow-up visits at the health center, I would not have met Nancy. If I hadn't met Nancy, another doctor, not Dr. B., probably would

> *We need to look for divine connections. We need to be present to acknowledge it.*

have removed the adhesions. I also would not have received the Christmas care I needed for the adhesion surgery. If I didn't have all of these wonderful people in my life, I don't know how I would have survived the surgeries, the treatments, and the recoveries.

It was amazing—amazing how fast it all came together and how one thing led to the other. And there was no question in my mind that it was the right thing. It all felt so right in my gut. It was like I had an inner guidance through the whole ordeal.

You should not blindly follow my lead...

Most new cancer patients are vulnerable and so afraid that they do anything the doctor says. If you find yourself in this position, you should not blindly follow my lead, but you should realize that there are many options available. Go forward. Be present. Listen to your inner guidance. Surround yourself with positive, supportive people. Do your research and take charge of your own medical care. There is hope. Define *your* protocol.

My protocol: Love, friendship, choices, positive thoughts, a strong boost to my immune system, and a healthy dose of divine intervention.

It's Complete

I am so thankful for my family and friends. Sometimes living single and alone can be isolating, sometimes scary. Sometimes I think, *This is it. I'm by myself.* But then I look up at the cross-stitch—the butterfly on my wall. It makes me happy. I remember Bari Ann and the transformations we went through. I remember Dr. Keller's love and support. I remember Nancy and the gifts she gave me—the gift of life, the gift of closure. I remember the divine intervention that wove its way through my journey, just like we all wove the thread of crosses through the fabric.

I didn't finish that cross-stitch myself, but there is a little piece of me in there—the imperfect part.

I didn't finish that cross-stitch myself, but there is a little piece of me in there—the imperfect part. I'll probably do another project someday, and that'll be the way I do it—by following my own rules. But I'll follow my gut, my inner guidance, and it will be okay.

The butterfly fan has so many memories—fearful, painful, loving, transformative memories. I've had it since the beginning of my cancer journey, and now I feel like it's complete. Kind of like where I am—I hope. That's what I believe and want to believe. I choose to think of my cancer journey as something really good that happened to me. I try to think positively in every situation. It's not easy, but it is part of *my* protocol.

The People in *My* Protocol

My protocol includes the love and unconditional support of positive family and friends. This butterfly could not have spread her wings without you.

Joe: Joe was and still is there for my boys. I am grateful for his support throughout such a difficult time in my life.

David: My kids mean the world to me. My eldest son has always been protective of me. He is my steadfast anchor. I am so proud of his artistic and entrepreneurial endeavors.

Derek: I'll say it again, my kids mean the world to me. My youngest son is our compassionate peacemaker. Although I miss him, I am so proud that he follows his inner compass and lives a free-spirited lifestyle—he is happy.

Evie: My instant granddaughter has been a source of joy for me. She was about six years old when I was diagnosed, and since then she has blossomed into a beautiful, confident, independent young woman.

Monica: Monica started the divine intervention ball rolling. Monica is a unique and trusted friend. I respect and care for her dearly.

Roger and Mary: As a result of my diagnosis, Roger and his wife, Mary, became my good friends during a tough season of my life. Roger introduced me to Dr. B., and for that I will be forever grateful. He never did agree with my treatment decisions, but he respected my wishes. Unfortunately, we lost contact after Joe and I divorced. Roger's cancer returned, and he passed away at the age of 82.

Dr. B.: His excellent bedside manner and conservative surgical approach put me at ease throughout both surgeries. I trusted him with my life.

Anne: Anne could always see right through me. I am so thankful that she had the courage to suggest I enroll in an Al-Anon program. I am even more thankful that God placed her in my path to tell me about Dr. Keller.

Valerie: Valerie is so knowledgeable, kind, and caring. She was an important link in the divine intervention chain of events. Valerie still owns a natural food store, and I visit her occasionally.

Bari Ann: What an amazing woman! She was patient and smart. I admired Bari Ann so much. In the grand scheme of life, we had little time together. But we made the most of the season that we did share. I felt so safe and welcome when I was in her presence. I loved Bari Ann as a sister, and I miss her dearly.

Dr. Keller: Dr. Keller was my rock through and after treatment. He always made me feel safe and loved. He was an attentive doctor with a special bedside manner. Even after my treatments ended, he helped me remember that my life is a gift that I need to live to the fullest.

Nancy: Nancy came into my life when I felt like I was on top of the world. I had beaten cancer, and I was ready to begin living my new life. But my world changed a couple of years ago, and thankfully, Nancy and Ethan were there for me. Through the years, Nancy has been a friend, a supervisor, a lifesaver, and a sister. I am forever grateful to Nancy and Ethan for their friendship, love, and support.

> *"'For I know the plans I have for you,' declares the Lord, 'plans to prosper you and not to harm you, plans to give you hope and a future.'"*
> Jeremiah 29:11

God: Throughout the years, my relationship with God has grown. I trust Him more. I listen to Him more. I see Him working through my life. He directs my path.

Me, Lynda: Yes, I am part of *my* protocol. I listen to my inner guidance, trust my gut, and make my own decisions. I am not perfect, and I am vulnerable at times. I enjoy spontaneous fun, but I take my time when it comes to my health. I surround myself with positive people, and I value each and every relationship. Like the cancer and the butterfly, I believe my transformation is complete.

Everyone Else Who Walked through This Journey with Me: If I did not specifically mention you in my story, please know that I have not forgotten about you. I cherish your help and support as well as our shared memories of this experience.

Postscript

During my research for this book, I came across the Annie Appleseed Project. Before she passed away, my friend Anne contributed to the content of this website (http://www.annieappleseedproject.org/). According to the site, "There are so many simple steps that can be taken to increase your chances of surviving and beating cancer. We want to help you make more informed treatment decisions."

I find this to be a fabulous resource, and I encourage readers to review the Annie Appleseed Project's information frequently.

Chronology of Events

1998: David and Alice plan their wedding. Lynda helps Alice with mother-of-the-bride activities. Lynda begins to see blood in her stool, but cancels colonoscopy.

1999: David and Alice marry. Lynda welcomes Alice and Evie into the family.

April 2000: Lynda sees her primary care physician (PCP) for a routine physical. She informs her PCP that she is tired and notices blood in her stool. PCP schedules a colonoscopy.

June 2000: Lynda completes the colonoscopy. The doctors immediately diagnose her with colorectal cancer. Lynda and Joe meet with the Salem, Massachusetts, surgeon the day after the colonoscopy. Monica calls Lynda that night and recommends that Lynda talks to Roger. Lynda calls Roger that night.

July 2000: Lynda consults with Dr. B. Her experience is completely different from her experience with the Salem, Massachusetts surgeon.

August 1, 2000: Dr. B. removes a low section of Lynda's colon and a few surrounding lymph nodes. Dr. B. informs Lynda of the *standard* protocol for *one* microscopic cancer cell found in *one* lymph node.

Late August 2000: Lynda visits three separate oncologists and receives the same *standard* protocol answer from all individuals.

Early September 2000: Lynda visits a Boston hospital cancer ward with Roger. Lynda reconnects with Anne and learns about Dr. Keller. Lynda emails Dr. Keller for the first time.

Late September 2000: Lynda tells Valerie and her yoga class about the Carnivora treatments. Valerie tells Lynda about Bari Ann. Lynda calls Bari Ann.

First Week of October 2000: Bari Ann and her mom, Selma, leave for Ireland for treatment.

October 8, 2000: Lynda and Joe travel to Ireland for treatment.

Late October 2000: Lynda continues treatment in the U.S. via self-injected liquid Carnivora. Lynda begins receiving follow up treatments at an alternative health center in Cambridge, Massachusetts. Lynda meets Nancy at the health center.

January 2001: Lynda begins working for Nancy at the health center as a staff nurse.

March 2001: Bari Ann purchases the cross-stitch project and gives it to Lynda.

April 2001: Lynda emails Dr. Keller with a follow up—she is feeling disconnected. Bari Ann is diagnosed with brain cancer.

April 28, 2003: Bari Ann passes away.

December 2012: Lynda experiences severe pain and undergoes small bowel obstruction emergency surgery. Nancy and Ethan welcome Lynda into their home for recovery and Christmas.

March 2013: Lynda asks Nancy for help completing the cross-stitch.

December 2013: Nancy finishes the cross-stitch project and gives it to Lynda as a Christmas gift.

January 2014: Lynda and Nancy purchase a frame for the cross-stitch project. They hang the project in Lynda's living room. This chapter of Lynda's life is finally complete.

Glossary

Many medical terms can be confusing and sometimes scary. I've done my best below to remove some of the mystery by explaining the term in my own words, but *please consult a physician or a medical dictionary for a precise definition.*

Carnivora: "A patented phytonutrient extract derived from the juice of the Venus Flytrap plant. Carnivora supplements mimic the body's own defense agents and support a stronger immune reaction." [ii] Carnivora is available in intravenous and pill form, but only the pill form is legal in the United States.

CAT scan: An imaging test that allows the doctor to see the inside of the body.

Chemotherapy: Treatment that uses drugs to stop or slow the growth of cancer cells.

Colon: Part of the digestive system. It is the top part of the large intestines—about four or five feet. It absorbs water and nutrients and then passes the remaining waste to the rectum.

Colorectal Cancer: Cancer of the colon and the rectum.

Colonoscopy: An outpatient procedure to examine the large bowel, which includes the colon and the rectum. The preparation for a colonoscopy is uncomfortable, but most patients are under light anesthesia during the procedure itself.

Colostomy: When the colon or rectum is not working correctly or is damaged, doctors might put an opening between the colon and the patient's skin. A bag is attached, and waste is eliminated through the bag.

Fascia: The strong connective tissue that surrounds all parts of the body. I think of it like cellophane. We are all like Spider-Man.

Hyperthermia: Hyperthermia treatments slowly and carefully raise the patient's body temperature— usually 105 to 109 degrees Fahrenheit. Hyperthermia treatments are only administered under the constant care of a medical professional. There are different types of hyperthermia treatments, including whole body, regional (a general area), or localized (a specific spot). Hyperthermia should not be confused with hypothermia, which implies a very low body temperature.

MRI (Magnetic Resonance Imaging): A test that uses a magnetic field and radio waves to create a picture of the inside of the body.

Radiation: Treatment that uses energy to kill cancer cells.

Rectosigmoid Cancer: A form of colorectal cancer, specifically, cancer of the junction between the rectum and sigmoid portion of the colon.

Rectum: The lower part of the large intestine that connects the colon to the anus.

Sigmoidoscopy: A procedure that the doctor can perform in the office to examine the lower colon. A lighted tube is inserted so the doctor can see inside the rectum. Anesthesia is not usually used during a sigmoidoscopy.

Endnotes

[i] Kuhl, David. "Chapter 2." *What Dying People Want: Practical Wisdom for the End of Life.* New York: Public Affairs, 2002. 33. Print.

[ii] "A Note From Dr. Keller." *A Note From Dr. Keller.* Carnivora Research Inc., International, 2010. Web. 22 May 2014. http://www.carnivora.com/note-from-dr-keller.html